QUOTES THAT EVERY **MAN** SHOULD LIVE BY

BY OUTSPOKEN MEN OF CALIBRE

This edition published in 2015 by Baker & Taylor UK Ltd,
Bicester,
Oxfordshire

© 2015 Susanna Geoghegan Gift Publishing
Collated by Michael Powell
Design by Milestone Design
Layout by Bag of Badgers
All rights reserved.

ISBN 978-1-910562-02-4

Printed in China.

INTRODUCTION

Every day the world bombards us with advice, mostly unwanted, from friends, parents, lovers and even strangers scrambling to share their preoccupations, prejudices and fears.

But did you know that the human brain – governed by the overriding imperative: 'Minimize danger, maximize reward' – is actually hardwired to mistrust advice?

Thankfully, this book is brimming with comical counsel you'll be delighted to read and maybe even to follow. It's a collection of funny and occasionally helpful lifestyle suggestions, all from men. You won't find a single woman among these pages because what do they know, right boys?

NEVER TRUST A MAN, WHO WHEN LEFT ALONE WITH A TEA COSY DOESN'T TRY IT ON.

BILLY CONNOLLY

THE ONLY PEOPLE WHO WEAR TIES DAILY ARE MALE POLITICIANS, REPORTERS AND DODGY ESTATE AGENTS.

JEREMY PAXMAN

Be content to remember that those who can make omelettes properly can do nothing else.

HILAIRE BELLOC

I DISTRUST CAMELS, AND ANYONE ELSE WHO CAN GO A WEEK WITHOUT A DRINK.

JOE E. LEWIS

WHEN YOU GO IN SEARCH OF HONEY YOU MUST EXPECT TO BE STUNG BY BEES.

JOSEPH JOUBERT

DON'T STICK YOUR TONGUE OUT UNLESS YOU INTEND TO USE IT.

DAVID LEE ROTH

If a woman tells you she's twenty and looks sixteen, she's twelve. If she tells you she's twenty-six and looks twenty-six, she's damn near forty.

CHRIS ROCK

NEVER TELL YOUR PROBLEMS TO ANYONE. TWENTY PER CENT DON'T CARE AND THE OTHER EIGHTY PER CENT ARE GLAD YOU HAVE THEM.

LOU HOLTZ

THE ENTIRE UNIVERSE HAS BEEN NEATLY DIVIDED INTO THINGS TO (A) MATE WITH, (B) EAT, (C) RUN AWAY FROM, AND (D) ROCKS.

TERRY PRATCHETT

Never tell a young person that anything cannot be done. God may have been waiting centuries for someone ignorant enough of the impossible to do that very thing.

G. M. TREVELYAN

I WOULD NEVER DIE FOR MY BELIEFS BECAUSE I MIGHT BE WRONG.

BERTRAND RUSSELL

ALWAYS GO TO THE BATHROOM WHEN YOU HAVE A CHANCE.

KING GEORGE V

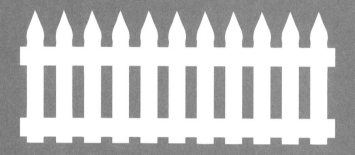

DON'T EVER TAKE A FENCE DOWN UNTIL YOU KNOW THE REASON IT WAS PUT UP.

G. K. CHESTERTON

IF YOU READ SOMEONE ELSE'S DIARY, YOU GET WHAT YOU DESERVE.

DAVID SEDARIS

Your time is limited, so don't waste it living someone else's life. Don't be trapped by dogma – which is living with the results of other people's thinking.

STEVE JOBS

MEMORISE QUOTES. THEY'RE USEFUL IN ENDING AND WINNING ARGUMENTS. THEN AGAIN, SO ARE SEMI-AUTOMATIC WEAPONS.

TONY DETHARIDGE

BEING IN LOVE CAN GIVE YOU SHORTNESS OF BREATH, PALPITATIONS, AND THE INABILITY TO CONCENTRATE. EXACTLY THE SAME SYMPTOMS AS CARBON MONOXIDE POISONING.

SEAN LOCK

Don't have sex, man. It leads to kissing and pretty soon you have to start talking to them.

STEVE MARTIN

PRACTICE MAKES PERFECT, BUT NOBODY'S PERFECT, SO WHY PRACTISE?

KURT COBAIN

YOU DON'T HAVE TO SWIM FASTER THAN THE SHARK, JUST FASTER THAN THE GUY NEXT TO YOU.

PETER BENCHLEY

PLAYING IT SAFE WILL ALWAYS END IN DISASTER.

BANKSY

STATISTICALLY SPEAKING, THERE IS A 65 PER CENT CHANCE THAT THE LOVE OF YOUR LIFE IS HAVING AN AFFAIR. BE VERY SUSPICIOUS.

SCOTT DIKKERS

Never play cards with a man named Doc. Never eat at a place called Mom's. Never sleep with a woman whose troubles are worse than your own.

NELSON ALGREN

DON'T TRY TO SOLVE SERIOUS MATTERS IN THE MIDDLE OF THE NIGHT.

PHILIP K. DICK

TALKING ABOUT MUSIC IS LIKE DANCING ABOUT ARCHITECTURE.

STEVE MARTIN

If you love two people at the same time, choose the second one, because if you really loved the first one you wouldn't have fallen for the second.

JOHNNY DEPP

TASTE EVERY FRUIT OF EVERY TREE IN THE GARDEN AT LEAST ONCE. IT IS AN INSULT TO CREATION NOT TO EXPERIENCE IT FULLY.

STEPHEN FRY

IF TWO WRONGS DON'T MAKE A RIGHT, TRY THREE.

LAURENCE J. PETER

IF YOU'RE GOING TO DO SOMETHING TONIGHT THAT YOU'LL BE SORRY FOR TOMORROW MORNING, SLEEP LATE.

HENNY YOUNGMAN

START EVERY DAY OFF WITH A SMILE AND GET IT OVER WITH.

W. C. FIELDS

Speak in French when you can't think of the English for a thing – turn your toes out when you walk – and remember who you are.

LEWIS CARROLL

IF YOU THINK A WEAKNESS CAN BE TURNED INTO A STRENGTH, I HATE TO TELL YOU THIS, BUT THAT'S ANOTHER WEAKNESS.

JACK HANDEY

FORGIVE YOUR ENEMIES, BUT NEVER FORGET THEIR NAMES.

JOHN F. KENNEDY

DON'T ASK ANYBODY ELSE IF THEY THINK YOU SHOULD DO IT. IF THEY KNEW IT WAS A GOOD IDEA THEY'D BE DOING IT.

SIMON WOODROOFE

Don't watch TV news. Look at those anchors in their wigs and ridiculous hairdos. Can you trust people who are lying about their appearance?

ERIC IDLE

YOU'RE SUPPOSED TO EAT THE COWS. THEY'RE GREAT BIG LUMBERING STUPID THINGS – THEY'D BE EVERYWHERE IF WE DIDN'T EAT THEM.

DYLAN MORAN

WHEN LIFE GIVES YOU LEMONS, CHUNK IT RIGHT BACK.

BILL WATTERSON

Don't do it! Stay away from your potential. You'll mess it up, it's potential, leave it. Anyway, it's like your bank balance – you always have a lot less than you think.

DYLAN MORAN

I'VE ALWAYS THOUGHT PEOPLE WOULD FIND A LOT MORE PLEASURE IN THEIR ROUTINES IF THEY BURST INTO SONG AT SIGNIFICANT MOMENTS.

JOHN BARROWMAN

THE BIGGEST CHALLENGE AFTER SUCCESS IS SHUTTING UP ABOUT IT.

CRISS JAMI

MAKE EVERYTHING AS SIMPLE AS POSSIBLE, BUT NOT SIMPLER.

ALBERT EINSTEIN

TROUSERS CAN NEVER BE TOO TIGHT. YOU HAVE TO GO THROUGH A COUPLE OF DAYS OF PAIN, THEN EVERYTHING STRETCHES OUT.

NOEL FIELDING

Don't put your trust in revolutions. They always come around again. That's why they're called revolutions. People die, and nothing changes.

TERRY PRATCHETT

THERE'S NO HALF-SINGING IN THE SHOWER, YOU'RE EITHER A ROCK STAR OR AN OPERA DIVA.

JOSH GROBAN

DON'T LOOK BACK – SOMETHING MIGHT BE GAINING ON YOU.

SATCHEL PAIGE

YOU CAN'T LEARN TOO SOON THAT THE MOST USEFUL THING ABOUT A PRINCIPLE IS THAT IT CAN ALWAYS BE SACRIFICED TO EXPEDIENCY.

W. SOMERSET MAUGHAM

Life is like a musical by Andrew Lloyd Webber – very popular and not as bad as some would have you believe – that is unspeakably awful but mercifully brief.

SIMON MUNNERY

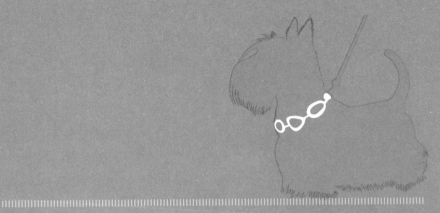

A DOG IS NOT INTELLIGENT. NEVER TRUST AN ANIMAL THAT'S SURPRISED BY ITS OWN FARTS.

FRANK SKINNER

MAKE NO MISTAKE ABOUT WHY THESE BABIES ARE HERE - THEY ARE HERE TO REPLACE US.

JERRY SEINFELD

You know I always assumed there would be a point when I would stop laughing at farts. It hasn't happened. I'm 35 years old and I haven't grown out of it.

JACK DEE

IN EVERY CIRCLE OF FRIENDS THERE'S ALWAYS THAT ONE PERSON EVERYONE SECRETLY HATES. DON'T HAVE ONE? THEN IT'S PROBABLY YOU.

WILL FERRELL

THE GREATEST THING YOU CAN DO IS SURPRISE YOURSELF.

STEVE MARTIN

ALWAYS DO SOBER WHAT YOU SAID YOU'D DO DRUNK. THAT WILL TEACH YOU TO KEEP YOUR MOUTH SHUT.

ERNEST HEMINGWAY

In the game of life, it's a good idea to have a few early losses, which relieves you of the pressure of trying to maintain an undefeated season.

BILL VAUGHAN

AVOID EMPLOYING UNLUCKY PEOPLE: THROW HALF OF THE PILE OF CVS IN THE BIN WITHOUT READING THEM.

DAVID BRENT (RICKY GERVAIS), THE OFFICE

ONE DOES NOT ALWAYS NEED A SCAPEGOAT, SOMETIMES A SCAPE TURKEY IS REQUIRED.

THOM THOMPSON

NEVER CRITICISE AMERICANS. THEY HAVE THE BEST TASTE THAT MONEY CAN BUY.

MILES KINGTON

HERE IS THE TEST TO FIND WHETHER YOUR MISSION ON EARTH IS FINISHED. IF YOU'RE ALIVE, IT ISN'T.

RICHARD BACH

A good night's sleep, or a ten-minute bawl, or a pint of chocolate ice cream, or all three together, is good medicine.

RAY BRADBURY

MY DAD USED TO SAY 'ALWAYS FIGHT FIRE WITH FIRE', WHICH IS PROBABLY WHY HE GOT THROWN OUT OF THE FIRE BRIGADE.

PETER KAY

THERE ARE ONLY TWO CONDITIONS WHERE YOU'RE ALLOWED TO WAKE UP A WOMAN ON A LIE-IN: IT'S SNOWING OR THE DEATH OF A CELEBRITY.

MICHAEL McINTYRE

If you're ridin' ahead of the herd, take a look back every now and then to make sure it's still there.

WILL ROGERS

YOU KNOW YOU MUST BE DOING SOMETHING RIGHT IF OLD PEOPLE LIKE YOU.

DAVE CHAPPELLE

NEVER PUT ANYTHING ON PAPER, MY BOY, AND NEVER TRUST A MAN WITH A SMALL BLACK MOUSTACHE.

P. G. WODEHOUSE

THERE IS A FINE LINE BETWEEN FISHING AND JUST STANDING ON THE SHORE LIKE AN IDIOT.

STEVEN WRIGHT

Don't bother just to be better than your contemporaries or predecessors. Try to be better than yourself.

WILLIAM FAULKNER

NO MAN SHOULD MARRY UNTIL HE HAS STUDIED ANATOMY AND DISSECTED AT LEAST ONE WOMAN.

HONORÉ DE BALZAC

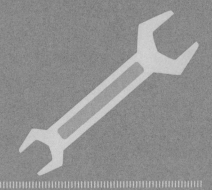

NEVER INVEST YOUR MONEY IN ANYTHING THAT EATS OR NEEDS REPAIRING.

BILLY ROSE

HIGH SCHOOL TAUGHT ME A VALUABLE LESSON ABOUT GLASSES: DON'T WEAR THEM. CONTACTS HAVE ALWAYS SEEMED LIKE TOO MUCH WORK, SO INSTEAD I JUST SQUINT, FIGURING THAT IF SOMETHING IS MORE THAN TEN FEET AWAY, I'LL JUST DEAL WITH IT WHEN I GET THERE.

DAVID SEDARIS

I believe you should place a woman on a pedestal – high enough so you can look up her dress.

STEVE MARTIN

NEVER PICK A FIGHT WITH AN UGLY PERSON; THEY'VE GOT NOTHING TO LOSE.

ROBIN WILLIAMS

IT'S SO SIMPLE TO BE WISE. JUST THINK OF SOMETHING STUPID TO SAY AND THEN DON'T SAY IT.

SAM LEVENSON

NEVER ATTRIBUTE TO MALICE THAT WHICH CAN BE ADEQUATELY EXPLAINED BY STUPIDITY.

ROBERT A. HEINLEIN

IT'S ALL RIGHT LETTING YOURSELF GO, AS LONG AS YOU CAN GET YOURSELF BACK.

MICK JAGGER

People who are fond of laws and sausages should not look too closely at how they are made.

OTTO VON BISMARCK

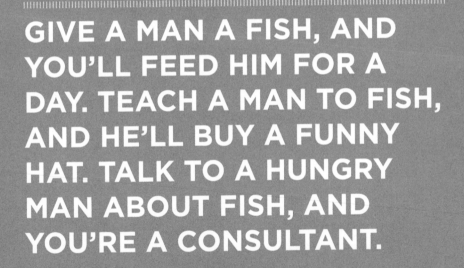

GIVE A MAN A FISH, AND YOU'LL FEED HIM FOR A DAY. TEACH A MAN TO FISH, AND HE'LL BUY A FUNNY HAT. TALK TO A HUNGRY MAN ABOUT FISH, AND YOU'RE A CONSULTANT.

SCOTT ADAMS

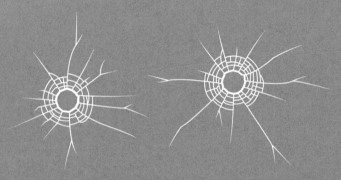

MUCH CAN BE ACCOMPLISHED WITH A SMILE. MORE CAN BE ACCOMPLISHED WITH A SMILE AND A GUN.

AL CAPONE

THE QUICKEST WAY TO DOUBLE YOUR MONEY IS TO FOLD IT OVER AND PUT IT BACK IN YOUR POCKET.

WILL ROGERS

You can live to be a hundred if you give up all the things that make you want to live to be a hundred.

WOODY ALLEN

DO NOT WORRY ABOUT AVOIDING TEMPTATION. AS YOU GROW OLDER IT WILL AVOID YOU.

JOEY ADAMS

ALWAYS BE WARY OF ANY HELPFUL ITEM THAT WEIGHS LESS THAN ITS OPERATING MANUAL.

TERRY PRATCHETT

BE SO GOOD THEY CAN'T IGNORE YOU.

STEVE MARTIN

There is one thing I have learned and that is not to dress uncomfortably, in styles which hurt: winklepicker shoes that cripple your feet and tight pants that squash your balls. Indian clothes are better.

GEORGE HARRISON

THAT'S THE BIG CHALLENGE OF LIFE – TO CHISEL DISAPPOINTMENT INTO WISDOM SO PEOPLE RESPECT YOU AND YOU DON'T ANNOY YOUR FRIENDS WITH YOUR WHINING.

MARC MARON

TRYING IS THE FIRST STEP TOWARDS FAILURE.

HOMER SIMPSON

AFTER A CERTAIN AGE EVERY MAN IS RESPONSIBLE FOR HIS FACE.

ALBERT CAMUS

When you find out the ultimate answer – be sure to act surprised.

BRADFORD FULLERTON

BUY LAND, THEY'RE NOT MAKING IT ANY MORE.

MARK TWAIN

IF YOU'VE ONLY KNOWN A GIRL FOR A WEEK OR TWO AND SHE INVITES YOU OVER TO LIGHT CANDLES AND HOLD HER IN YOUR ARMS FOREVER . . . SHE MISSES HER EX-BOYFRIEND.

DAVE COMPETELLO

HITLER WAS A VEGETARIAN. JUST GOES TO SHOW: VEGETARIANISM, NOT ALWAYS A GOOD THING. CAN, IN SOME EXTREME CASES, LEAD TO GENOCIDE.

BILL BAILEY

NEVER TAKE NOTICE OF ANONYMOUS LETTERS, UNLESS YOU GET A FEW THOUSAND ON THE SAME SUBJECT.

ROBERT MENZIES

Don't bite off more than you can chew because nobody looks attractive spitting it back out.

CARROLL BRYANT

MY ADVICE? YOU WANNA LOOK TWENTY YEARS YOUNGER? STAND FURTHER AWAY.

JEFF GREEN

NEVER EXAGGERATE YOUR FAULTS. YOUR FRIENDS WILL ATTEND TO THAT.

FRANCIS BACON

He who disagrees with me in private, call him a fool. He who disagrees with me in public, call him an ambulance.

SIMON MUNNERY

YOU CAN STUMP ANY STONER WITH ONE QUESTION: WHAT WERE WE JUST TALKING ABOUT?

JIM BREUER

A LESSON TO BE LEARNED FROM YOUR DOG: ONCE YOU URINATE ON SOMETHING, IT'S YOURS FOREVER.

CHRISTOPHER JOHNSON

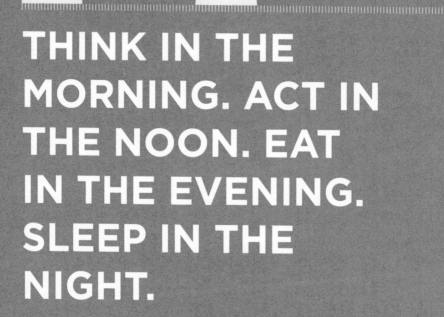

THINK IN THE MORNING. ACT IN THE NOON. EAT IN THE EVENING. SLEEP IN THE NIGHT.

WILLIAM BLAKE

THE SECRET TO ENJOYING YOUR JOB IS TO HAVE A HOBBY THAT'S EVEN WORSE.

BILL WATTERSON

Always watch where you are going. Otherwise, you may step on a piece of the Forest that was left out by mistake.

A. A. MILNE

NEVER, UNDER ANY CIRCUMSTANCES, TAKE A SLEEPING PILL AND A LAXATIVE ON THE SAME NIGHT.

DAVE BARRY

IT'S ALWAYS FUNNY UNTIL SOMEONE GETS HURT. THEN IT'S JUST HILARIOUS.

BILL HICKS

Dire Straits is a great band. Someone tells you they like 'Brothers in Arms' and immediately you know they're a stupid annoying git.

ALEXEI SAYLE

LAZINESS IS THE MOTHER OF ALL BAD HABITS BUT ULTIMATELY SHE IS A MOTHER AND WE SHOULD RESPECT HER.

SHIKAMARU NARA

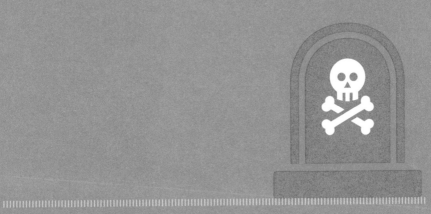

EVERYBODY GOING TO BE DEAD ONE DAY, JUST GIVE THEM TIME.

NEIL GAIMAN

IN AN UNDERDEVELOPED COUNTRY DON'T DRINK THE WATER. IN A DEVELOPED COUNTRY DON'T BREATHE THE AIR.

JONATHAN RABAN

TO ACHIEVE GREAT THINGS, TWO THINGS ARE NEEDED: A PLAN AND NOT QUITE ENOUGH TIME.

LEONARD BERNSTEIN

Don't be chuckin' stuff about, if you're surrounded by glass an' what have ya.

KARL PILKINGTON

ALL PERSONS, LIVING AND DEAD, ARE PURELY COINCIDENTAL.

KURT VONNEGUT

ALWAYS GO TO OTHER PEOPLE'S FUNERALS, OTHERWISE THEY WON'T COME TO YOURS.

YOGI BERRA

DRINK THE FIRST. SIP THE SECOND SLOWLY. SKIP THE THIRD.

KNUTE ROCKNE

If you're being chased by a police dog, try not to go through a tunnel, then on to a little seesaw, then jump through a hoop of fire. They're trained for that.

MILTON JONES

THE AMERICAN DREAM IS A CROCK. STOP WANTING EVERYTHING. EVERYONE SHOULD WEAR JEANS AND HAVE THREE T-SHIRTS, EAT RICE AND BEANS.

BILL HICKS

NEVER REFUSE WINE. IT IS AN ODD BUT UNIVERSALLY HELD OPINION THAT ANYONE WHO DOESN'T DRINK MUST BE AN ALCOHOLIC.

P. J. O'ROURKE

You can't put a
price tag on love.
But if you could,
I'd wait for it to
go on sale.

JAROD KINTZ

NEVER GIVE IN TO
PEER PRESSURE,
ESPECIALLY IF
THE PEER IS NOT
ATTRACTIVE.

EUGENE MIRMAN

*NEVER LET YOUR SENSE
OF MORALS PREVENT
YOU FROM DOING
WHAT IS RIGHT.*

ISAAC ASIMOV

IF AT FIRST YOU DON'T SUCCEED, DESTROY ALL EVIDENCE THAT YOU TRIED.

STEVEN WRIGHT

I THINK THAT MEN OUGHT TO TREAT WOMEN LIKE SOMETHING OTHER THAN WEAKER MEN WITH BREASTS.

JIM BUTCHER

If a person offends you, do not resort to extremes, simply watch your chance and hit him with a brick.

MARK TWAIN

ALWAYS BEHAVE LIKE A DUCK – KEEP CALM AND UNRUFFLED ON THE SURFACE BUT PADDLE LIKE THE DEVIL UNDERNEATH.

JACOB BRAUDE

I BELIEVE THAT IF LIFE GIVES YOU LEMONS, YOU SHOULD MAKE LEMONADE . . . AND TRY TO FIND SOMEBODY WHOSE LIFE HAS GIVEN THEM VODKA, AND HAVE A PARTY.

RON WHITE

WHY BE DISAGREEABLE, WHEN WITH A LITTLE EFFORT YOU CAN BE IMPOSSIBLE?

DOUGLAS WOODRUFF

THE ONLY GOOD THING TO DO WITH GOOD ADVICE IS PASS IT ON; IT IS NEVER OF ANY USE TO ONESELF.

OSCAR WILDE

My advice for a person who's just fallen out of a skyscraper window is, flap your arms . . . faster.

JAROD KINTZ

I GOT THE BLUES THINKING OF THE FUTURE, SO I LEFT OFF AND MADE SOME MARMALADE. IT'S AMAZING HOW IT CHEERS ONE UP TO SHRED ORANGES AND SCRUB THE FLOOR.

D. H. LAWRENCE

MONEY CAN'T BUY YOU LOVE, BUT IT CAN GET YOU SOME REALLY GOOD CHOCOLATE GINGER BISCUITS.

DYLAN MORAN

Quotes are for dumb people who can't think of something intelligent to say on their own.

BO BURNHAM

THE WAY I FIGURE IT, IF YOU CAN'T TELL I'M HIGH BY LOOKING AT ME, I WIN.

MARC MARON

BATH TWICE A DAY TO BE REALLY CLEAN, ONCE A DAY TO BE PASSABLY CLEAN, ONCE A WEEK TO AVOID BEING A PUBLIC MENACE.

ANTHONY BURGESS

DANCE LIKE IT HURTS. LOVE LIKE YOU NEED MONEY. WORK WHEN PEOPLE ARE WATCHING.

SCOTT ADAMS

If you're going to make a science fiction movie, then have a hovercraft chase, for God's sake.

JOSS WHEDON

ONLY DUMB PEOPLE TRY TO IMPRESS SMART PEOPLE. SMART PEOPLE JUST DO WHAT THEY DO.

CHRIS ROCK

LIFE IS A WHIM OF SEVERAL BILLION CELLS TO BE YOU FOR A WHILE.

GROUCHO MARX

ALWAYS BE NICE TO THOSE YOUNGER THAN YOU, BECAUSE THEY ARE THE ONES WHO WILL BE WRITING ABOUT YOU.

CYRIL CONNOLLY

Never trust any complicated cocktail that remains perfectly clear until the last ingredient goes in, and then immediately clouds.

TERRY PRATCHETT

I DON'T BELIEVE IN AN AFTERLIFE, BUT I'M TAKING AN EXTRA PAIR OF UNDERWEAR JUST IN CASE.

WOODY ALLEN

THERE ARE TWO TYPES OF PEOPLE IN THIS WORLD. PEOPLE WHO HATE CLOWNS . . . AND CLOWNS.

D. J. MACHALE

IF AT FIRST YOU DON'T SUCCEED, FIND OUT IF THE LOSER GETS ANYTHING.

WILLIAM LYON PHELPS

The greatest and most important problems of life are all fundamentally insoluble. They can never be solved but only outgrown.

CARL JUNG

IF YOU CAN DO A HALF-ASSED JOB OF ANYTHING, YOU'RE A ONE-EYED MAN IN A KINGDOM OF THE BLIND.

KURT VONNEGUT

IF PEOPLE TURN TO LOOK AT YOU ON THE STREET, YOU ARE NOT WELL DRESSED.

BEAU BRUMMEL

What looks good now is guaranteed to embarrass you twenty years down the line, which is, of course, the whole problem with fashion.

DAVID SEDARIS

IF YOU DON'T GO FISHING BECAUSE YOU THOUGHT IT MIGHT RAIN YOU WILL NEVER GO FISHING. THIS APPLIES TO MORE THAN FISHING.

GARY SOW

BEWARE OF ALL ENTERPRISES THAT REQUIRE NEW CLOTHES.

HENRY DAVID THOREAU

IF YOU COULD KICK THE PERSON IN THE PANTS RESPONSIBLE FOR MOST OF YOUR TROUBLE, YOU WOULDN'T SIT FOR A MONTH.

THEODORE ROOSEVELT

I think you should be a child for as long as you can. I have been successful for 74 years being able to do that. Don't rush into adulthood, it isn't all that much fun.

BOB NEWHART

HARD WORK PAYS OFF IN THE FUTURE. LAZINESS PAYS OFF NOW.

STEVEN WRIGHT

NEVER STAND BETWEEN A DOG AND THE HYDRANT.

JOHN PEERS

WE HAVE NOTHING TO FEAR BUT FEAR ITSELF. THAT, AND THOSE GREAT BIG FURRY SPIDERS.

LEV L. SPIRO

THERE IS ALMOST NO MARITAL PROBLEM THAT CAN'T BE HELPED ENORMOUSLY BY TAKING OFF YOUR CLOTHES.

GARRISON KEILLOR

You should be as alive as you can, until you're totally dead.

DYLAN MORAN

LEAVE THE HOUSE BEFORE YOU FIND SOMETHING WORTH STAYING IN FOR.

BANKSY

NEVER INSULT SEVEN MEN IF YOU'RE ONLY CARRYING A SIX SHOOTER.

HARRY MORGAN

IT IS BETTER TO BE QUOTABLE THAN TO BE HONEST.

TOM STOPPARD

Sometimes, when I'm feeling down because nothing seems to be going right, I like to take a home pregnancy test. Then I can say, 'Hey, at least I'm not pregnant.'

DANIEL TOSH

WHEN YOU'RE IN JAIL, A GOOD FRIEND WILL BE TRYING TO BAIL YOU OUT. A BEST FRIEND WILL BE IN THE CELL NEXT TO YOU SAYING, 'DAMN, THAT WAS FUN.'

GROUCHO MARX

IF YOU ONLY EVER READ ONE BOOK IN YOUR LIFE, I HIGHLY RECOMMEND YOU KEEP YOUR MOUTH SHUT.

SIMON MUNNERY

IF SOMEONE OFFERS YOU A BREATH MINT, ACCEPT IT.

H. JACKSON BROWN, JR.

As far as I'm concerned, if something is so complicated that you can't explain it in 10 seconds, then it's probably not worth knowing anyway.

BILL WATTERSON

COMFORT HAS ITS PLACE, BUT IT SEEMS RUDE TO VISIT ANOTHER COUNTRY DRESSED AS IF YOU'VE COME TO MOW ITS LAWNS.

DAVID SEDARIS

OLDER PEOPLE SHOULDN'T EAT HEALTH FOOD, THEY NEED ALL THE PRESERVATIVES THEY CAN GET.

ROBERT ORBEN

HONESTY IS
ALWAYS GOOD,
EXCEPT WHEN IT'S
BETTER TO LIE.

JAMES PATTERSON

Always borrow
money from a
pessimist. He won't
expect it back.

OSCAR WILDE

84

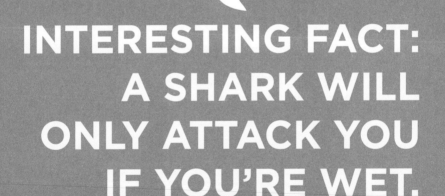

INTERESTING FACT: A SHARK WILL ONLY ATTACK YOU IF YOU'RE WET.

SEAN LOCK

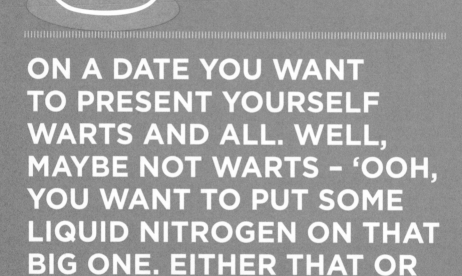

ON A DATE YOU WANT
TO PRESENT YOURSELF
WARTS AND ALL. WELL,
MAYBE NOT WARTS – 'OOH,
YOU WANT TO PUT SOME
LIQUID NITROGEN ON THAT
BIG ONE. EITHER THAT OR
A HAT.'

RUSSELL KANE

THE BEST WAY TO REMEMBER YOUR WIFE'S BIRTHDAY IS TO FORGET IT ONCE.

E. JOSEPH COSSMAN

My dad said, 'Always leave them wanting more.' Ironically, that's how he lost his job in disaster relief.

MARK WATSON

LET A SMILE BE YOUR UMBRELLA, AND YOU'LL END UP WITH A FACE FULL OF RAIN.

GEORGE CARLIN

SOMETIMES THE ROAD LESS TRAVELLED IS LESS TRAVELLED FOR A REASON.

JERRY SEINFELD

DON'T TRY TO HOG LONELINESS AND KEEP IT ALL TO YOURSELF. SHARE IT WITH A SPECIAL SOMEONE.

JAROD KINTZ

'It's not whether you win or lose, it's how you play the game', according to the losers and their parents.

BUSTER GURU

THERE'S ONLY FOUR THINGS YOU CAN BE IN LIFE: SOBER, TIPSY, DRUNK AND HUNGOVER. TIPSY IS THE ONLY ONE WHERE YOU DON'T CRY WHEN YOU'RE DOING IT.

JAMES ACASTER

GROW ANGRY SLOWLY - THERE'S PLENTY OF TIME.

RALPH WALDO EMERSON

TO BEGIN, BEGIN.

WILLIAM WORDSWORTH

There are two days in the week about which and upon which I never worry. Two carefree days, kept sacredly free from fear and apprehension. One of these days is Yesterday and the other day I do not worry about is Tomorrow.

ROBERT JONES BURDETTE

I HAVE SOMETHING THAT I CALL MY GOLDEN RULE. IT GOES SOMETHING LIKE THIS: 'DO UNTO OTHERS TWENTY-FIVE PER CENT BETTER THAN YOU EXPECT THEM TO DO UNTO YOU' . . . THE TWENTY-FIVE PER CENT IS FOR ERROR.

LINUS PAULING

A LARGE, CLUMSY UMBRELLA IS THE BEST PROTECTION AGAINST THE RAIN: THERE WILL BE NO RAIN AS LONG AS YOU'RE LUGGING IT AROUND.

PETER WASTHOLM

ALWAYS LIVE IN THE UGLIEST HOUSE ON THE STREET – THEN YOU DON'T HAVE TO LOOK AT IT.

DAVID HOCKNEY

You should laugh everywhere you can find even the slightest glimmer of humour.

DOUG STANHOPE

EVERYONE HAS A PURPOSE IN LIFE. PERHAPS YOURS IS WATCHING TELEVISION.

DAVID LETTERMAN

REMEMBER THAT THE MOST BEAUTIFUL THINGS IN THE WORLD ARE THE MOST USELESS; PEACOCKS AND LILIES FOR INSTANCE.

JOHN RUSKIN

IN LIFE, IT'S NOT WHO YOU KNOW THAT'S IMPORTANT, IT'S HOW YOUR WIFE FOUND OUT.

JOEY ADAMS

If you have a chance to drive a tank, do it. Because when are you going to be able to drive a tank again?

JEFF SCOTCH

IF YOU EVER DROP YOUR KEYS INTO A RIVER OF MOLTEN LAVA, LET 'EM GO, BECAUSE MAN, THEY'RE GONE.

JACK HANDEY

EAT A LIVE FROG FIRST THING IN THE MORNING AND NOTHING WORSE WILL HAPPEN TO YOU THE REST OF THE DAY.

MARK TWAIN

I try to avoid having thoughts. They lead to other thoughts, and – if you're not careful – those lead to actions. Actions make you tired. I have this on rather good authority from someone who once read it in a book.

BRANDON SANDERSON

IF YOU EVER FALL OFF THE SEARS TOWER, JUST GO REAL LIMP, BECAUSE MAYBE YOU'LL LOOK LIKE A DUMMY AND PEOPLE WILL TRY TO CATCH YOU BECAUSE, HEY, FREE DUMMY.

JACK HANDEY

NO! TRY NOT. DO, OR DO NOT. THERE IS NO TRY.

YODA, STAR WARS

WHEN FACING A DIFFICULT TASK, ACT AS THOUGH IT IS IMPOSSIBLE TO FAIL. IF YOU ARE GOING AFTER MOBY DICK, TAKE ALONG THE TARTARE SAUCE.

WALTER SMITH

ALWAYS AND NEVER ARE TWO WORDS YOU SHOULD ALWAYS REMEMBER NEVER TO USE.

WENDELL JOHNSON

When you go in for a job interview, I think a good thing to ask is if they ever press charges.

JACK HANDEY

FOLLOW YOUR DREAMS, EXCEPT FOR THE ONE WHERE YOU'RE NAKED IN CHURCH.

REV. DAVID AULT

IT'S IMPOSSIBLE TO BE UNHAPPY IN A PONCHO.

NOEL FIELDING

DON'T EVER GET YOUR SPEEDOMETER CONFUSED WITH YOUR CLOCK, LIKE I DID ONCE, BECAUSE THE FASTER YOU GO, THE LATER YOU THINK YOU ARE.

JACK HANDEY

Here's what you do: you pick up your guitar, you rip a few people's tunes off, you swap them round a bit, get your brother in the band, punch his head in every now and again, and it sells.

NOEL GALLAGHER

IF YOU'RE NOT PART OF THE SOLUTION, YOU'RE PART OF THE PRECIPITATE.

STEVEN WRIGHT

STICKING FEATHERS UP YOUR BUTT DOES NOT MAKE YOU A CHICKEN.

CHUCK PALAHNIUK

NEVER MOON A WEREWOLF.

MIKE BINDER

Never give up on your dreams because most people who never gave up on theirs actually never achieved them and died broke, lonely and miserable. But you shouldn't let that stop you.

BUSTER GURU

MY FORMULA FOR LIFE IS VERY SIMPLE: IN THE MORNING, WAKE UP; AT NIGHT, GO TO SLEEP. IN BETWEEN I TRY AND OCCUPY MYSELF AS BEST I CAN.

CARY GRANT

ALL YOU NEED IS LOVE. BUT A LITTLE CHOCOLATE NOW AND THEN DOESN'T HURT.

CHARLES M. SCHULZ

If you ever have trouble opening a bottle of champagne, my advice – hit it with a ship. I've seen people do that. It works.

PAUL F. TAYLOR

YOU MUST LEARN FROM THE MISTAKES OF OTHERS. YOU CAN'T POSSIBLY LIVE LONG ENOUGH TO MAKE THEM ALL YOURSELF.

SAM LEVENSON

A DISHONEST MAN YOU CAN ALWAYS TRUST TO BE DISHONEST.

JOHNNY DEPP

I DON'T WATCH TELEVISION. IT DESTROYS THE ART OF TALKING ABOUT ONESELF.

STEPHEN FRY

IT MAY BE WINTER OUTSIDE, BUT IT'S ALWAYS SUMMER IN YOUR ARMPIT.

TOMMY GORMAN

People who are always looking over their shoulder will most likely run into something.

CHARLES HUFFINE

NEVER TRUST A MAN WITH SHORT LEGS . . . HIS BRAIN'S TOO NEAR HIS BOTTOM.

NOEL COWARD

DON'T JUMP ON A MAN UNLESS HE'S DOWN.

FINLEY PETER DUNNE

I DO NOT ADVOCATE VIOLENCE. I ADVOCATE PEACE. AND THEN JUST WHEN MY OPPONENT BELIEVES ME, I PUNCH HIM IN THE FACE.

BUSTER GURU

The only way to spend New Year's Eve is either quietly with friends or in a brothel. Otherwise when the evening ends and people pair off, someone is bound to be left in tears.

W. H. AUDEN

SPEAK SOFTLY AND EMPLOY A HUGE MAN WITH A CROWBAR.

TERRY PRATCHETT

WHATEVER YOU HEAR AT THE BARBER SHOP, STAYS AT THE BARBER SHOP.

BERNIE MAC

YOU SHOULDN'T BE EATING ANYTHING THAT TAKES SIX MINUTES TO MICROWAVE.

ADAM CAROLLA

Beware of undertaking too much at the start. Be content with quite a little. Allow for accidents. Allow for human nature, especially your own.

ARNOLD BENNETT

CLEANLINESS IS NEXT TO GODLINESS. AND THE CHIP SHOP IS NEXT TO THE HAIRDRESSER'S. IT DOESN'T PERSUADE ME TO VISIT EITHER.

SIMON MUNNERY

BE RESPECTFUL TO YOUR SUPERIORS, IF YOU HAVE ANY.

MARK TWAIN

Anybody who says they are a good liar obviously is not, because any legitimately savvy liar would always insist they're honest about everything.

CHUCK KLOSTERMAN

DON'T BUY ONE OF THOSE BABY MONITORS. BABIES PRETEND TO BE DEAD. THEY'RE BASTARDS AND THEY DO IT ON PURPOSE.

BILLY CONNOLLY

MEN ARE FROM EARTH, WOMEN ARE FROM EARTH. DEAL WITH IT.

GEORGE CARLIN

NEVER MEMORISE SOMETHING THAT YOU CAN LOOK UP.

ALBERT EINSTEIN

When trouble arises and things look bad, there is always one individual who perceives a solution and is willing to take command. Very often, that individual is crazy.

DAVE BARRY

WHEN YOU LOOK IN THE MIRROR AND DESPAIR AND NONE OF YOUR CLOTHES SEEM APPROPRIATE, RELAX. PUT THE KETTLE ON. IT MIGHT SUIT YOU.

SIMON MUNNERY

NEVER WRITE A LETTER IF YOU CAN HELP IT, AND NEVER DESTROY ONE.

JOHN A. MACDONALD

DON'T MESS WITH A WIZARD WHEN HE'S WIZARDING!

JIM BUTCHER

WHEN LIFE GETS YOU DOWN, JUST REMEMBER THESE THREE WORDS OF WISDOM: 'BONK!', 'ZAP!', AND 'YOWSERS!'.

TYLER WEBB

Look to the future, because that is where you'll spend the rest of your life.

GEORGE BURNS

IF YOU WANT TO CONFUSE A GIRL, BUY HER A PAIR OF CHOCOLATE SHOES.

MILTON JONES

INSTEAD OF WONDERING WHEN YOUR NEXT VACATION IS, MAYBE YOU SHOULD SET UP A LIFE YOU DON'T NEED TO ESCAPE FROM.

SETH GODIN

Never give in! Never give in! Never, never, never, never – in nothing great or small, large or petty. Never give in except to convictions of honour and good sense.

WINSTON CHURCHILL

IF YOU CAN'T BEAT THEM, ARRANGE TO HAVE THEM BEATEN.

GEORGE CARLIN

IT'S EASIER TO PUT ON SLIPPERS THAN TO CARPET THE WHOLE WORLD.

AL FRANKEN

I'VE NEVER WORKED OUT WHAT THE MORAL OF HUMPTY DUMPTY IS. I CAN ONLY THINK OF: DON'T SIT ON A WALL IF YOU'RE AN EGG.

RICKY GERVAIS

NEVER EXPRESS YOURSELF MORE CLEARLY THAN YOU ARE ABLE TO THINK.

NIELS BOHR

Never try to keep up with the Joneses. Drag them down to your own level. It is ever so much cheaper.

QUENTIN CRISP

IF EVERYTHING SEEMS TO BE GOING WELL, YOU HAVE OBVIOUSLY OVERLOOKED SOMETHING.

STEVEN WRIGHT

ALWAYS TELL THE TRUTH. YOU MAY MAKE A HOLE IN ONE WHEN YOU'RE ALONE ON THE GOLF COURSE.

FRANKLIN P. JONES

Honesty may be the best policy, but it's important to remember that apparently, by elimination, dishonesty is the second-best policy.

GEORGE CARLIN

I THINK, IN MOST CASES, THE DIFFERENCE BETWEEN DEPRESSION AND DISAPPOINTMENT IS YOUR LEVEL OF COMMITMENT.

MARC MARON

RULE ONE OF PLAYING IT COOL: ONLY SMILE AT HER FACE.

JEFF MURDOCK (RICHARD COYLE), COUPLING

IF YOU WANT TO SURVIVE IN LIFE, YOU'VE GOT TO KNOW WHERE YOUR TOWEL IS.

DOUGLAS ADAMS

When you are lonely, and feel like you don't have a friend in the world, just remember: people tend to avoid people who are like that.

BUSTER GURU

NOBODY CAN BE BAD AT EVERYTHING. THERE'S NO SUCH THING AS A PERFECT SCREWUP.

JIM BUTCHER

I HAVE ALWAYS DRESSED ACCORDING TO CERTAIN BASIC GUY FASHION RULES, INCLUDING: BOTH OF YOUR SOCKS SHOULD ALWAYS BE THE SAME COLOUR OR THEY SHOULD AT LEAST BOTH BE FAIRLY DARK.

DAVE BARRY

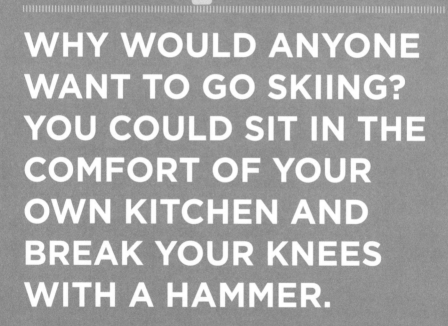

WHY WOULD ANYONE WANT TO GO SKIING? YOU COULD SIT IN THE COMFORT OF YOUR OWN KITCHEN AND BREAK YOUR KNEES WITH A HAMMER.

DYLAN MORAN

THE SMALLER THE MONKEY THE MORE IT LOOKS LIKE IT WOULD KILL YOU AT THE FIRST GIVEN OPPORTUNITY.

PETER KAY

The important thing is not to stop questioning . . . Never lose a holy curiosity.

ALBERT EINSTEIN

STICKS AND STONES MAY BREAK MY BONES, BUT WORDS WILL ALWAYS HURT ME.

STEPHEN FRY

PEOPLE WHO READ THE TABLOIDS DESERVE TO BE LIED TO.

JERRY SEINFELD

WHEN YOU ENCOUNTER SEEMINGLY GOOD ADVICE THAT CONTRADICTS OTHER SEEMINGLY GOOD ADVICE, IGNORE THEM BOTH.

AL FRANKEN

There are two kinds of people in this world: those who believe there are two kinds of people in this world and those who are smart enough to know better.

TOM ROBBINS

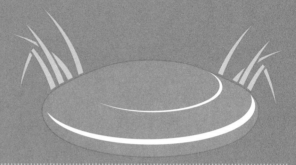

IT'S IMPOSSIBLE TO LOOK COOL WHILST PICKING UP A FRISBEE.

PETER KAY

THE MEAL IS NOT OVER WHEN I'M FULL. THE MEAL IS OVER WHEN I HATE MYSELF.

LOUIS C. K.

YOU'RE ONLY GIVEN A LITTLE SPARK OF MADNESS. YOU MUSTN'T LOSE IT.

ROBIN WILLIAMS

Never get married in college; it's hard to get a start if a prospective employer finds you've already made one mistake.

ELBERT HUBBARD

WHEN A GIRL SAYS SHE WANTS TO BE FRIENDS WITH BENEFITS, I ALWAYS ASK IF THAT INCLUDES DENTAL INSURANCE.

JAROD KINTZ

131

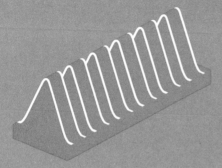

TOBLERONES! IT'S IMPOSSIBLE TO EAT A TOBLERONE WITHOUT HURTING YOURSELF.

BILLY CONNOLLY

THE BEST WORK NEVER WAS AND NEVER WILL BE DONE FOR MONEY.

JOHN RUSKIN

Desperation is a necessary ingredient to learning anything, or creating anything. Period. If you ain't desperate at some point, you ain't interesting.

JIM CARREY

IF YOU ARE DOING THINGS THE SAME WAY AS TWO YEARS AGO, YOU ARE ALMOST CERTAINLY DOING THEM WRONG.

JOHN HARVEY-JONES

I'D RATHER BE HAPPY THAN RIGHT.

MARCUS BRIGSTOCKE

THERE'S NOTHING WRONG WITH BEING SHALLOW AS LONG AS YOU'RE INSIGHTFUL ABOUT IT.

DENNIS MILLER

Remember that the most important thing is to try and love other people as much as they love you.

DAVID SEDARIS

NEVER READ A POP-UP BOOK ABOUT GIRAFFES.

SEAN LOCK

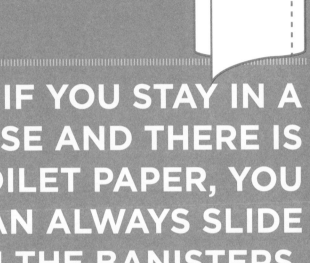

IF YOU STAY IN A HOUSE AND THERE IS NO TOILET PAPER, YOU CAN ALWAYS SLIDE DOWN THE BANISTERS. DON'T TELL ME YOU HAVEN'T TRIED IT.

PAUL MERTON

WHEN A BANKER JUMPS OUT OF A WINDOW, JUMP AFTER HIM - THAT'S WHERE THE MONEY IS.

ROBESPIERRE

There is one other reason for dressing well, namely that dogs respect it, and will not attack you in good clothes.

RALPH WALDO EMERSON

IF YOU THINK YOUR BOSS IS STUPID, REMEMBER: YOU WOULDN'T HAVE A JOB IF HE WAS ANY SMARTER.

JOHN GOTTI

EXPECT THE UNEXPECTED. AND WHENEVER POSSIBLE, BE THE UNEXPECTED.

JACK DORSEY

THE SAFE AND CULTURAL METHOD OF EATING CRACKERS IN BED IS TO WEAR A DIVER'S SUIT INSTEAD OF PYJAMAS.

BASIL WOLVERTON

I REALISED THAT TO COMPARE YOUR INSIDES WITH OTHER PEOPLE'S OUTSIDES LEADS TO UNHAPPINESS.

MARCUS BRIGSTOCKE

If you can keep your son off the pipe and your daughter off the pole, you're ahead of the game.

CHRIS ROCK

NEVER TRUST ANYBODY WHO SAYS 'TRUST ME'. EXCEPT JUST THIS ONCE, OF COURSE.

JOHN VARLEY

HALF OF SEEMING CLEVER IS KEEPING YOUR MOUTH SHUT AT THE RIGHT TIMES.

PATRICK ROTHFUSS

BIOLOGICALLY SPEAKING, IF SOMETHING BITES YOU, IT IS MORE LIKELY TO BE FEMALE.

DESMOND MORRIS

Humour keeps us alive. Humour and food. Don't forget food. You can go a week without laughing.

JOSS WHEDON

WHATEVER STORY YOU'RE TELLING, IT WILL BE MORE INTERESTING IF AT THE END YOU ADD, 'AND THEN EVERYTHING BURST INTO FLAMES'.

BRIAN P. CLEARY

IT IS BETTER TO BE A PIRATE THAN TO JOIN THE NAVY.

STEVE JOBS

The first time you see something that you have never seen before, you almost always know right away if you should eat it or run away from it.

SCOTT ADAMS

BEFORE YOU MARRY A PERSON YOU SHOULD FIRST MAKE THEM USE A COMPUTER WITH SLOW INTERNET TO SEE WHO THEY REALLY ARE.

WILL FERRELL

TIME YOU ENJOY WASTING, WAS NOT WASTED.

JOHN LENNON

IF YOU DON'T GET EVERYTHING YOU WANT, THINK OF THE THINGS YOU DON'T GET THAT YOU DON'T WANT.

OSCAR WILDE

A good plan isn't one where someone wins, it's where nobody thinks they've lost.

TERRY PRATCHETT

THE THING ABOUT QUOTES ON THE INTERNET IS YOU CANNOT CONFIRM THEIR VALIDITY.

ABRAHAM LINCOLN